The Little E

The focus in this book is on past tense verbs.

Verbs ending with -ed

jumped   croaked
wobbled   floated
groaned   landed
reached   crashed
looked   toppled
soaked   bleated
turned

Verbs ending with -ing

watching   having
leaving

Jelly was watching a pair of robins having a fight over a worm, when she saw a little blue boat in the lake.

Jelly went to the boat. She jumped in it. Then she saw a toad. The toad croaked. The boat wobbled. Jelly held on.

The boat floated away from the bank. It wobbled from side to side. 'Oh no,' groaned Jelly. 'I want to get out.'

Jelly held on tight as the boat floated up the lake. A big fish jumped out of the water and the boat wobbled again.

Jelly held on tighter when the big fish landed back in the water. 'Oh no,' groaned Jelly. 'I want to get out!'

The boat reached the bank at the far side of the lake. Jelly could see her chance. She could get out now.

She took a huge leap just as the boat crashed into the bank. She landed safely on the grass, leaving the toad in the boat.

Jelly looked up. A grumpy goat was right in front of her. 'Oh no,' groaned Jelly. 'Where is the boat? I want to get in.'

She turned round and leapt for the boat. The boat wobbled from side to side. Then it completely toppled over.

Jelly was now wet through in the water. She was soaked. The toad croaked at her and the goat bleated at her. Hmmph!

Words with digraphs and trigraphs used in this book

ay/ai:	away again
a-e:	lake safely
ee/ea:	reached leap leaving bleated
ie/i-e:	side
igh:	fight tight tighter right
oa:	boat toad croaked floated
	groaned goat soaked
oo:	took looked
ou/ow:	out round now
er:	over water tighter her
ar:	far
aw:	saw
ue/u-e:	blue huge
ur:	turned
air:	pair